A Year On The Farm

First published in the great Britain 2002 by Brimax.
An imprint of Octopus Publishing Group Ltd
2-4 Heron Quays, London, E14 4JP

ISBN 1-85854-308-8

A CIP catalogue record for this book is available from the British Library.

Created and produced by Linda Watters

Illustrated by Lisa Alderson and Simon Mendez

Design by Andrew Crowson

Indexing and glossary by Hazel Burgess

Printed in China

A Year on the Farm

Written by
Linda Watters

Illustrated by
Lisa Alderson & Simon Mendez

BRIMAX

Contents

Introduction

You will probably have eaten a sandwich before. Maybe it had butter, or margarine on it. It could have been made with cheese, banana, or bacon. You might have washed it down with a glass of cold milk!

These are foods and drinks that we have almost every day, but have you ever thought about where they come from? Almost all of the food we eat will have started life on the farm. If farmers did not grow wheat, we would not have delicious fresh bread, or yummy cereal for breakfast!

There are different types of farms, and farmers need to carry out many jobs at different times of the year. Winter is the time for getting the land ready to plant the crops that will be harvested the following summer or autumn.

Imagine if you could spend a whole year on the farm and watch all the things that happen with the changing of the seasons. On the following pages you will discover what happens on the farm, starting from the first bloom of spring, until the end of winter, when it starts all over again!

Types of farms

There are many different kinds of farms all over the world. Years ago, farms were mixed, which meant they grew crops and raised animals. Today, most farms are specialised, which means they produce only one or two main types of crops, or one or two types of animals.

Any farm that keeps and raises animals is called a livestock farm.

Cattle farms
These farms keep and raise cattle for their meat. There are different types of cattle and very often each farm will keep just one or two types.

Dairy farms
A dairy farm keeps cows (female cattle) for milking. The cows are milked twice a day, all year round, and the milk is used to make dairy products.

Sheep farms
These farms keep lambs and sheep for meat and wool. Again, there are many different types of sheep and each farm will usually keep just one or two types.

Pig farms
A pig farm is another livestock farm that raises animals for meat. In some countries you may see pigs out in the fields. In other countries pigs are kept inside, in stalls.

Types of farms

Poultry farms

Poultry farms keep birds, like chickens, geese, and ducks, for their meat, eggs, and feathers.

Chicken farms

There are two kinds of chicken farms. "Free-range" farms are where the birds are allowed to roam free in the yard.

There are also "factory farms", where the birds are kept inside. These farms keep more birds and produce more food.

Ducks and geese
Ducks and geese do not like to be kept inside so they are usually kept on free-range farms. They are farmed for eggs and meat, and their feathers are used to make bedding, like quilts and pillows.

Turkey farms
Turkeys are farmed on both free-range and factory farms. They provide us with meat all year round, but the busiest harvest is at Christmas.

Ostrich farms
There are farms that keep and raise ostriches for meat, eggs, and feathers. Some of the biggest farms are in Africa, where the bird comes from, but they are now also farmed in the US, Australia, and Europe.

Types of farms

Crop farms

These farms grow only grain crops, like **wheat** and **barley**. They have lots of large fields which need to be looked after all year round. Crop farms often grow only one or two types of crops.

Fruit farms

Fruit farms all over the world grow different types of fruit all year round. Most farms grow only one or two kinds of fruit, depending on the weather. Oranges, lemons, and bananas need to grow in hot countries. Apples, pears, and berries can be farmed in cooler places.

Vegetable farms

These farms grow only vegetables, such as potatoes, beans, and carrots. Most vegetables grow outside in the fields, but some also grow inside green houses or plastic tunnels.

Other farms

There are also farms that grow only trees and flowers, or keep fish. There are many farms that keep and farm other things, like deer for meat, bees for honey, and even snails that can be eaten.

Farm buildings

The buildings needed on a farm, and how they are used, will depend on the type of farming that is carried out. A dairy farm needs milking sheds, a cattle farm needs cow sheds, while a crop farm will need barns to store crops. These are some of the main buildings you will see around different farms.

The farmhouse

The farmhouse is where the farmer and his or her family live. It is usually at the centre of the farm, surrounded by the other buildings in the farmyard.

Barns
Barns are buildings that are used for storing crops, animal food, or keeping animals. Many barns, which were once used for storing crops, are now used to store farm machinery.

Open-sided barn
Some farms store hay and straw in an open-sided barn, so that air can flow through. This helps keep the crop dry.

Cattle yards and barns
During the winter, cattle are brought indoors to yards or barns, where they are kept warm and dry. The farmer will feed them with hay, or special animal food, and give them straw to sleep on.

Farm buildings

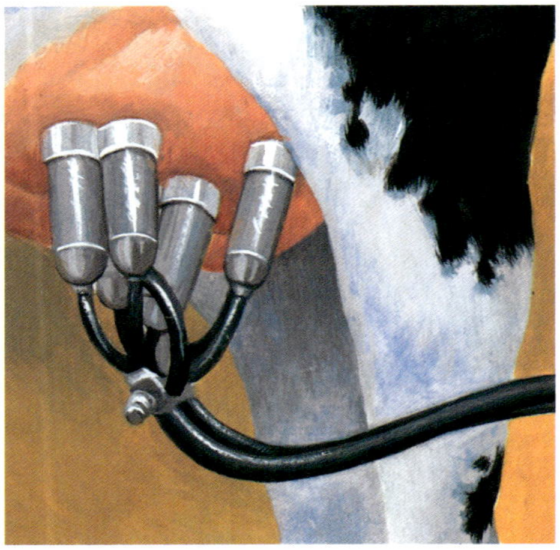

Milking parlour

On a dairy farm, the milking parlour is the most important building. The cows are brought into a milking stall, where the milking machine is attached to the udder. The milk is taken by pipes and tubes to a large tank where it is kept cool.

Chicken coop

Some chickens are kept outdoors, but they need a place where they can lay eggs, sleep, and get shelter. It is called a chicken coop, or a hen house. It usually has wheels on the bottom so it can be moved to fresh ground.

Silo

Food for the animals is stored in a silo. These can be seen on most farms and they look like tall round towers, but they can also be buried underground in pits.

Farm Facts

Farmers used to make holes in the roofs of barns so owls would nest inside. This helped keep rats and mice away from the crop.

Years ago, many farms only had one building. The family lived at one end, and the animals lived at the other.

Farm machinery

Before the invention of machinery, farmers used horses, oxen, and simple tools on the farm. Today, machines make farming easier, which means farmers can produce much more food. Different types of farms need different machinery, but one machine you will always see on a farm is a **tractor**.

Tractors
Modern tractors are very large and very powerful. They can operate two machines at the same time, and they can lift very heavy weights, such as bales of hay.

The plough
Before crops can be planted, the field must be ploughed to get rid of weeds and break up the soil. The first plough was made of wood and pulled by horses, or oxen. Today, ploughs are made from steel, and pulled behind a tractor.

Rollers

Once the soil has been ploughed, it is flattened using a roller. This breaks down any lumps of earth and leaves behind a smooth surface. Today, rollers are pulled behind tractors, but years ago teams of horses would pull them.

The harrow

Just before planting, the farmer pulls a harrow over the field. This breaks up the soil and makes it light and crumbly. Modern harrows are made from steel and pulled behind a tractor.

Farm machinery

Seed drill
The first seed drill looked like a wooden wheelbarrow. It had a sharp blade, which cut through the soil, with a tube attached to it. The seeds were dropped into the soil through the tube. Modern seed drills have many blades and many tubes for seeds.

Combine harvester
Years ago, many tools and lots of people were needed for the harvest. Today the combine harvester does all the jobs of the harvest. It cuts the crop and removes the useful part from the waste. The grain is stored in the combine harvester, before being poured into a trailer, and the waste is dropped onto the ground.

Sprayers

Farmers need to protect the growing crop from pests and disease. They do this by spraying chemicals over the crop using a machine called a sprayer. It has long arms, called booms, with nozzles attached to them.

Spreaders and hoppers

Farmers use spreaders and hoppers to spread fertilizer over the field. Animal manure is spread over the crop using a machine called a “manure spreade”

Farm Facts

The first rollers were made from large, heavy, tree trunks.

Early farmers used branches of trees and sticks to plough the soil.

Preparing the soil

In spring, one of the first things a crop farmer has to do is get the soil ready so that crops can grow. Seeds do not like soil that is hard or has stones or weeds in it. Getting the soil ready for planting is called **tilling**.

Many years ago, farmers would till the soil using sticks and rakes.

Later, they used **ploughs** and **harrows**, which horses or oxen would pull.

Today, ploughs and harrows are pulled by tractors.

The plough cuts through the soil and turns it over, so that the weeds are buried and new soil comes to the top. This is called a **furrow**.

This freshly ploughed soil is still not ready for planting. The farmer now needs to prepare a **seed bed**. This is done with a harrow, which the farmer drags across the field, behind the tractor.

Sowing the seeds

Once the soil is ready, the farmer must plant the seeds. Modern farmers use a machine called a **seed drill**. Years ago, the seeds would be planted by hand. People would walk up and down the fields, either scattering the seed, or using a stick called a **dibber**. They would stab a hole in the soil and drop the seed in.

The seed drill works much faster because it can sow many rows of seeds at one time. It has lots of tubes that each have a sharp knife at the end. They cut small trenches in the soil, and the seeds are dropped down through the tubes. Modern farmers call this "drilling the seed".

After the seed is drilled, the field is rolled to make sure the soil is pressed down around the seed.

The seeds are now left to grow, but the farmer needs to take care of them and protect them from wildlife, insects, weeds, and disease.

Farm Facts

Some farms still use scarecrows to keep the birds from stealing the seeds.

Years ago, school children were used as "bird scarers". They would run up and down the fields all day, making lots of noise!

Feeding and protecting the crops

All crops need lots of warm sunshine and water to make them grow. The farmer also needs to make sure that they are getting enough food from the soil, and do not get destroyed by wildlife or disease.

Some farmers put **manure** on the crops to help them grow. Manure is made from animal dung mixed with straw.

Most farmers use **fertilizers**, which have chemicals in them. These chemicals kill weeds that threaten the crop. Other sprays poison insects. Some of these chemicals are very dangerous and to use them the farmer has to follow special rules.

The chemical fertilizers are sprayed over the field by a spraying machine that has long arms called "booms" with nozzles attached.

Farms that have a large area to cover, for example in the US and in Australia, often use aeroplanes for spraying.

The good news is that chemical fertilizers help farmers grow much more food.

The bad news is that some of the chemicals can leak into our streams and rivers, causing **pollution**, which is harmful to all living things, including humans.

Farm Facts

In many places, farmers are not allowed to spray in a high wind because this could carry the chemicals and be harmful to people and wildlife.

Some farms do not use chemical fertilizers. They are called **organic farms**.

Main types of crops

The crops that a farmer plants depend on the type of soil, weather conditions, and also what the farmer can sell. Below are some of the most common crops planted around the world.

Wheat

Wheat is the most important arable crop, because most people eat it daily. The grain of the wheat is turned into flour, which is then made into bread. Wheat is also used to make breakfast cereal and pasta. It grows like tall grass and turns yellow when it is ready.

Barley

Barley grain is used to make different foods, like breakfast cereals or soup. Barley also goes into making whiskey and beer. The long stems of barley turn gold when they are ripe and ready.

Corn

Native Americans were the first people ever to grow corn. Corn is also known as maize, and it is grown all over the world. The best corn is eaten as corn-on-the-cob, sweetcorn, breakfast cereal, or popcorn. Some of the crop will make oil and food for animals.

Potatoes
The potato is a crop that most countries plant and there are many different types. Potatoes are a very important crop because they can be eaten in many different ways, from mashed potatoes to french fries and potato crisps.

Sugar beet
A sugar beet plant has green leaves and knobbly roots. The root of the plant is called the beet, and this is where the sugar comes from. Sugar also comes from sugar cane, which only grows in hot countries.

Canola seed
Canola is grown mostly to make oils for cooking and margarine spreads. As soon as the yellow flowers die away at the end of spring, the seeds are ready to be harvested. The canola seed is crushed and squeezed to get the oil out.

Cattle farming

In spring, cows are ready to give birth to their calves. As soon as they have given birth, they are put out into the fields, with their calves, to graze on the fresh grass. Only female cattle are called cows, male cattle are called bulls.

Cows do not have any top front teeth, but they do have four stomachs. They eat grass by wrapping their tongues around it and pulling it up out of the ground into their mouths.

After the cow eats the grass, it is swallowed and goes into the cow's first stomach, where the food is stored and broken down into smaller pieces, called cud. When the cow has finished grazing, some of the grass she has eaten is brought back into her mouth. She chews it again until it is soft and mushy. This is called "chewing the cud".

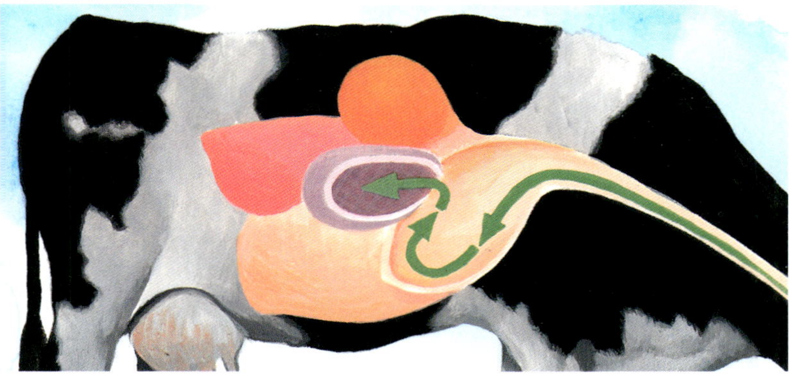

The cud is then swallowed and it goes into the second stomach where it is stored.

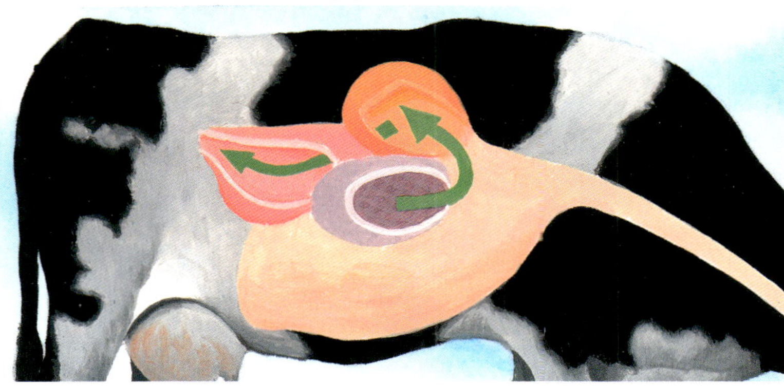

After a while the food passes into the third and fourth stomach where it is finally digested.

The farmer also gives the cows cattle feed, which helps protect them from disease.

Cattle are usually kept in groups called **herds**. Herds kept for milking are called **dairy cattle**. Herds kept for meat are called **beef cattle**.

Farm Facts

Cows are **herbivores**, animals that eat plants instead of meat.

Cows need to drink at least 25 gallons of water every cay. That could almost fill a bathtub!

Dairy cattle

A **dairy farm** is where a herd of cows is kept just for making milk. Milk is picked up from the dairy every day and taken to factories where it is put into bottles or cartons. It is also made into other foods, such as cheese, butter, or ice cream. These are known as dairy products.

A cow is called a **heifer** until her first calf is born. A cow will only produce milk once she has had a calf.

It is very important that a cow is milked often. If not, her milk will dry up. Milking takes place twice a day, early in the morning and again in the afternoon. A cow will keep producing milk for about ten months.

Years ago, cows were milked by hand and the milk was contained in a bucket. Milking by hand was very slow work!

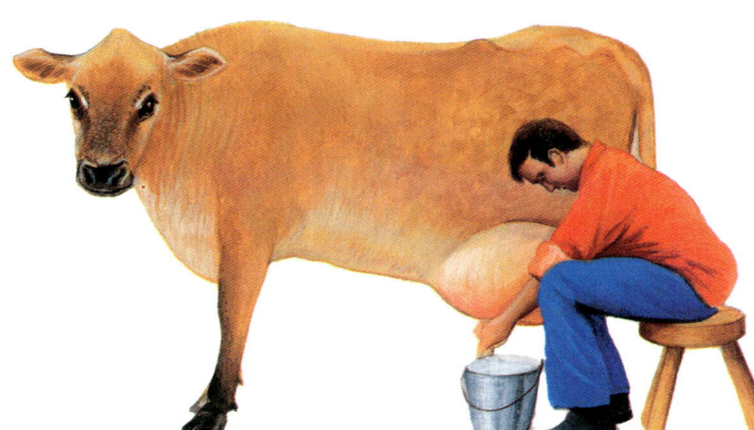

Today, machines in a building called the milking parlour do the milking.

Each cow goes into a space, called a stall, where the milking machine is attached to the udders.

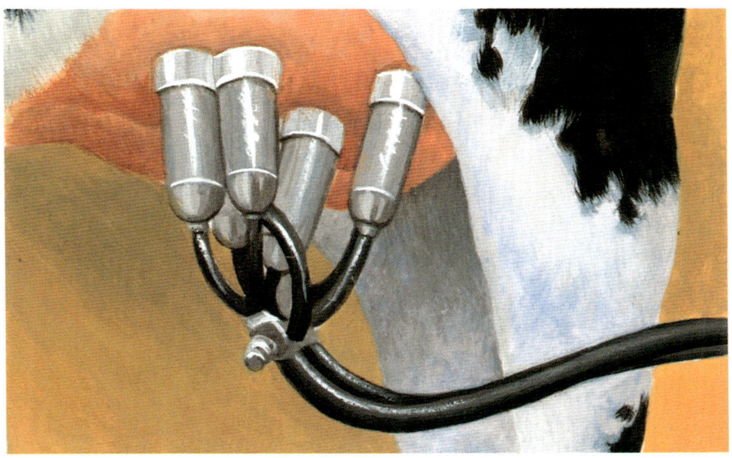

The milk goes along tubes and from the machines into glass jars.

From here it goes into a large tank, where it is kept cool.

After milking, the cows go back out into the field again while the milking parlour is cleaned to get ready for next time!

Farm Facts

Every herd has a "queen cow" who takes the lead when the herd moves.

Cows lick their skin and flick their tails to brush off dirt or insects.

Sheep farming

Most sheep live outdoors in the fields or on hills all year round. Sheep who live on hills have extra thick coats and can run very fast. Lowland sheep are usually fatter and slower. In spring, the female sheep, called **ewes**, are ready to give birth to their lambs.

The lambs will be born out in the field, unless the ewe needs help with the birth.

The shepherd, or farmer, keeps a close watch on the sheep when they are due to give birth. If all is well, the ewe will feed the lamb. Sometimes, if the lamb is sick or the ewe doesn't want to feed it, the lamb will be bottle-fed.

Farm Facts

In Australia, there are ten times more sheep than people.

Sheep's milk is also used to make cheese.

Young lambs spend their days out in the fields with their mothers. Like cows, sheep have an extra stomach and eating grass keeps them healthy. The farmer does not need to give them extra food in the spring, but he must still keep watch over them.

A male sheep is called a **ram**, and a group of sheep is called a **flock**. A specially trained dog, called a sheepdog, helps to round them up. Sheepdogs are so smart that they sometimes take part in competitions.

Maple syrup farming

Have you ever wondered where the maple syrup that you eat on pancakes comes from? Most of the maple syrup we eat comes from Canada and the US. The Native Americans were the first people to **tap** maple trees for their **sap** to make sugar and syrup.

Syrup and sugar are made from sap, which is the sticky liquid that runs up from the roots and all through the tree.

Sugaring starts with the tapping of the maple trees in early spring. The sap runs when the weather during the day is above freezing, and the weather at night is below freezing.

Farmers make a tap in the tree to get the sap out. A tap is a hole about 5 cm. deep in the bark of the tree.

Some farms may still collect the sap in buckets, but most farms use pipes and tubes, which run from each tree to a large tank where the sap is collected.

Farm Facts

Each tap can produce two pints of syrup in four weeks.

Sap is turned into syrup by boiling away the water.

Maple trees can live, and be tapped, for up to 300 years, but they need to be a certain size before they can be tapped. This means they are not tapped until they are at least 30 to 40 years old.

Soil and water

Crops need lots of fresh water to make them grow. In the summer months, the weather can be hot and dry, so making sure the crops are well watered is an important task for some farmers. In times of little rainfall, farmers must use stored water.

Rainwater collects underground and creates wells of water. This is taken along pipes or channels to the fields. The water can also be sprayed over the crops using a sprinkler. This is called **irrigation**.

If the climate is very hot, the soil can become too dry and can blow away in the wind.

It can also be washed away by heavy rain.

This is called **soil erosion**.

In the 1930s, there was a long drought in part of the US.

The soil was so dry that it blew away. The crops would not grow and the farmers had to leave the land. This land was useless for many years and became known as the "Dust Bowl".

Farm Facts

Older farms were usually built near a water supply, such as a pond or river.

Cutting down forests also causes soil erosion. Without the trees for protection, the soil is blown or washed away.

Making hay

Hay making takes place early in the summer months. Rain can destroy the hay crop, so it has to be **harvested**, dried, and stored quickly. This is where the old saying “Make hay while the sun shines,” comes from.

Before the invention of machines, the hay crop would be cut by hand, using a tool called a **sickle**, or a tool called a **scythe**.

Hay is dried grass, which is cut down before it has flowered, and then left to dry in the sun. This hay is used as bedding and to feed animals during the winter.

Years ago, once the hay was dry, it was piled onto a cart using a long-handled pitch fork.

Today, the **combine harvester** makes the hay into big round or rectangular bales. The bales are stored in a barn, which has open sides to let the air through.

Farm Facts

In Roman times, hay was harvested by hand using a scythe.

The first sickle was made in Stone Age times from flint.

Harvesting cereal crops

Once the crop has grown and ripened, it is time for the harvest to begin. Years ago, the crop was harvested by hand, which was very long and hard work. Today, with modern machinery, the harvest is finished much quicker and farmers can produce more food.

In the past, the crop was cut using a sickle, or a scythe, and then tied into bundles, or **sheaves**.

After drying out, the crop had to be **threshed** (beaten to get the grain out). The stalks would be hit with a wooden stick called a **flail**, to knock the grain off.

Once the grain was collected it was tossed up in the air to get rid of the dust. This was called **winnowing**.

Later, a steam-powered threshing machine was invented to separate the grain.

Today, farmers have the combine harvester, which does all the harvesting jobs at once.

A combine harvester is so called because it combines all the functions of the harvest. It separates the useful part of the crop from the waste, called straw.

Farmers who keep livestock will use this straw for bedding in the winter.

Farm Facts

Wheat is the world's biggest cereal crop. It is grown mostly in North America.

Rice is the world's second biggest cereal crop. It is grown mostly in Asia.

Fruit farming

As part of a healthy diet, we need to eat lots of fruit, so farmers all over the world grow different types of fruit all year round. The different **climates** around the world mean that fruit is always growing, or being harvested, in some country.

The type of fruit grown, and the time of harvest, will depend on the climate. In Florida, USA, there is an orange harvest in winter.

Citrus fruits, such as oranges and lemons, need lots of sunshine to grow. They are grown in hot countries, such as the US, Spain, and South Africa. Peaches and apricots also need plenty of sunshine.

Exotic fruit, like bananas and pineapples, are grown all year round in tropical areas, such as Asia, Australia, South America, and Africa.

Soft fruits, such as strawberries, raspberries, cherries, and plums, grow more widely in cooler parts of the world.

Peaches and most other soft fruits are picked by hand in summer. This means the fruit will not get damaged during the harvest.

Farm Facts

Bananas do not grow on trees. They grow in bunches on the stems of large plants.

The first peaches were found growing wild in China.

Vegetable farming

Some farmers grow only vegetables. These farms tend to be smaller, but they need more people to work on them, to pick the vegetables by hand and take care of the crops.

Fast-growing vegetables, such as carrots and potatoes, are planted in the spring and are ready to be harvested at different times from mid- to late-summer.

During the summer months farmers check the crops, to make sure they are growing well.

It is important that insects and disease are not allowed to attack the crops.

Some plants are grown inside greenhouses, and planted out in the fields in summer.

Farm Facts

A machine is used to harvest peas, and it even pops the peas out of their pods!

Tomatoes are often picked when they are green. They ripen and turn red on the way to market.

Farmers can fight any pests or disease that may attack the crop by spraying it with chemicals. Some vegetable farmers prefer to use only organic methods, which make the food more expensive but healthier.

Weeds are bad news because they steal water, sunshine, and food from the plants.
Farmers need to dig and turn the soil between the rows of vegetables to keep any weeds from taking root.

Many crops are harvested by hand, because machinery can damage some types of vegetables. Machines pulled by tractors harvest root vegetables, such as potatoes.

Sheep farming

Sheep are well-protected and kept warm by their woolly coats, but during the summer months they become too hot. This is when the farmer brings them down to the farm to be **sheared** and dipped.

The coat of the sheep, called the **fleece**, is cut off using electric clippers. It takes skill to get the fleece off in one whole piece. With electric clippers, a sheep can be sheared in less than a minute.

Before electric clippers were invented, sheep were sheared using hand-held shears.

In countries where they have very large flocks of sheep, such as Australia and New Zealand, skilled "shearing gangs" travel from farm to farm, shearing sheep all day.

The fleeces are an important crop for the farmer. They are twisted into tight bundles, packed into a sack, and sold to make wool.

The sheep also have a bath to kill off any insects or diseases that they have. This bath contains special chemicals and it is called a sheep dip. The whole sheep must be fully dipped for a few seconds. Most farmers dip their sheep twice a year.

Farm Facts

The world record for sheep shearing is 89 in one hour.

Goats are also farmed for fleeces, which make very expensive wool.

At the end of the summer, the lambs are **weaned** from their mothers. This means that instead of drinking their mother's milk, they will be fed by the farmer.

Cattle farming

Cattle spend the summer months in the field grazing on the fresh grass, but the farmer still needs to take care of them, and give them extra food. The herd also has to be checked for any signs of disease or illness.

The **veterinary surgeon** will treat any animals that are sick, and give the whole herd medicine, to prevent them from catching common illnesses.

Cows are pregnant for ten months. In the summer, they become pregnant with the calves that will be born the following spring.

On large cattle farms in the US, the cattle are moved to new grazing fields so they have fresh grass to eat. This is called a "cattle drive" and lots of cowhands on horses will help round up the cattle and move them to new pastures. It is a very noisy and dusty job!

Summer is also the time for making hay, which will feed the cows, or be used as bedding in the winter.

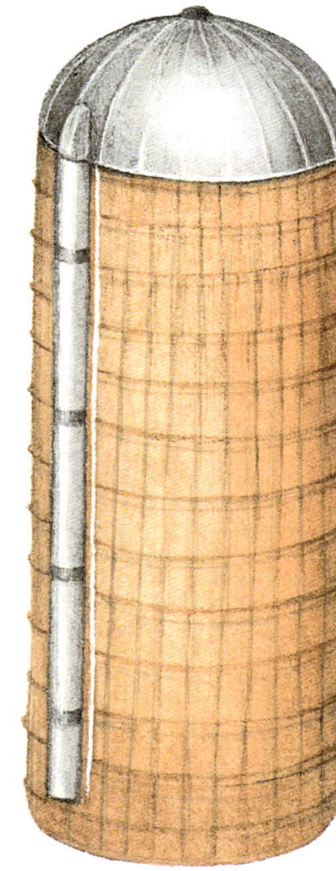

Some farmers will make **silage** for animal food. The grass is stored in an airtight container, called a pit or **silo**, while it is still green. Making silage uses the natural chemicals in the grass.

Farm Facts

India has more cattle than any other country.

All cattle are "branded" or "ear-tagged" with a special mark or number.

Agriculture fairs

Late summer is the time when many countries hold farm shows and agriculture fairs. These shows bring together all different people from the farming community, where they take part in competitions, displays, play games, and just have fun.

The shows are usually held on farm land and there are many tents and stalls with refreshments and crafts.

There are often pet shows at the fair, and the winners are given special ribbons for first, second, and third place.

There are lots of animals on show, such as horses, cows, goats, pigs, and chickens.

There are displays of vegetables and flowers, and judges who choose the winners.

It is a great place to see farm machinery up close. Tractors, ploughs, harrows, combine harvesters, and even old steam engines are on display.

The farm show is an important event for the farming community. It brings everyone together so they can talk about their farming year and have some fun!

Preparing the ground

After the harvest the crop farmer needs to till the soil and get it ready for planting again. In the autumn, the farmer will plant crops that will be harvested the following spring or summer.

A plough or harrow is dragged over the field attached to the back of a tractor. This turns up the fresh soil and gets rid of any weeds.

The field is then rolled to make a seed bed.

Wheat can be planted in the autumn or spring. Wheat planted in the autumn is called "winter wheat". It grows more slowly than wheat planted in the spring, but it gives a much larger crop.

The seeds used to be planted by hand, but now they are planted using a seed drill. This is why farmers often say “drilling the seed” instead of “planting the seed”.

Farm Facts

When the soil is crumbly and ready for planting it is called **tilth**.

Some harrows, called disc harrows, have circular blades instead of spikes.

Harvesting vegetables

Some crops, like potatoes, sugar beets, and corn, are harvested in the autumn. Potatoes used to be harvested by hand until a special "potato plough" was invented. Today, most vegetables are harvested by a machine, which is pulled behind a tractor.

The harvesting machine digs out the rows and brings the potatoes up to the surface. The part of the plant we know as the potato is called the **tuber**.

Sugar comes from the root of the plant, called the "beet". It is very knobbly and can grow to the size of a football. The beet is taken to special factories where the sugar is taken out. The left-over green leaves of the plant are used to make animal feed.

Corn is grown to make animal feed, but it is also grown to make oil, breakfast cereal, and popcorn. Before the combine harvester was invented, the crop would be cut and collected by hand, which was very slow and hard work.

Farm Facts

Native Americans were the first people ever to grow corn and potatoes.

Today potatoes are produced to make the very best potato crisps .

Cattle farming

Towards the end of the autumn, the cattle are brought in from the fields and hills. They are checked by the vet and treated for any illness, before being put into barns, where they will be kept warm and dry, and be fed, through the winter months.

The cows and calves are kept in separate buildings so the calves have to be weaned from their mothers. This means that the farmer will feed them.

They are fed twice a day, with silage in the morning, and straw or hay at night.

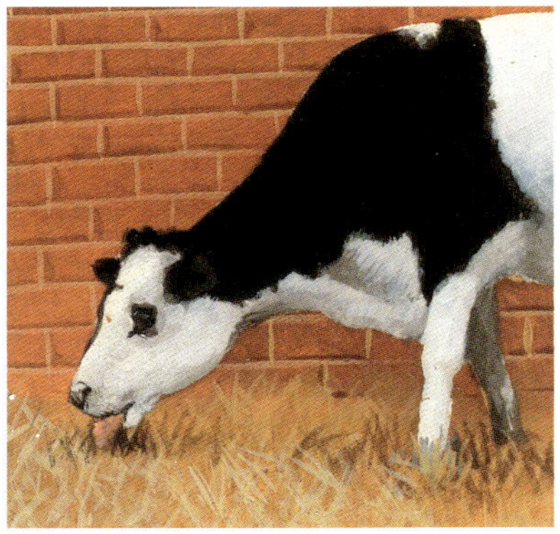

The calves and cows will also have the hair on their heads and backs clipped to keep them cool.

Farm Facts

Shaggy, long-haired, Scottish Highland cows can have calves until they are 17 years old.

The ancient Egyptians were one of the first people to farm cattle.

On many large farms in the US, the cattle are rounded up and driven into fenced **corrals** close to the ranch or farm buildings. Any cows that are pregnant are kept close to the farm so the farmer can keep watch over them.

Sheep farming

In the autumn, the farmer moves the sheep and lambs to new grazing fields or hills. They are checked by the vet and given medicine to keep them from getting diseases. They may also be "dipped" in a chemical bath to get rid of any insects.

Instead of drinking milk from their mothers, the lambs will be fed by the farmer.

Some of the female lambs, called ewe lambs, will stay on the farm and become part of the main flock.

Any extra ewe lambs and all the male lambs, called "wedder lambs", are taken to the market to be sold. Before they go to the market their belly and tail wool is sheared.

In some parts of the world, sheep farms have hills. The lambs born on one part of the hill, called a **heft**, will live there for about five years. The farmer will put a different-coloured mark on the sheep so he knows which heft they come from.

Farm Facts

On huge sheep farms in Australia and New Zealand, some farmers use motorcycles to round up the sheep.

Some sheep farms are so huge they cover an area the size of a large city.

Poultry farming

Chickens, ducks, geese, and turkeys are all poultry. They are farmed mostly for eggs and meat. Goose and duck feathers are also used to make bedding, such as pillows and quilts.

Some poultry flocks are allowed to roam freely around the farmyard, pecking at weeds and insects. The farmer also feeds them on scraps and spare grain. This is called "free-range" farming.

Free-range chickens need a chicken coop, or house, where they lay and sit on their eggs. They are also shut in here at night to protect them from foxes.

Farm Facts

Hens do not fly. They can only flap and flutter up and down.

Hens eat grain, insects, and scraps. In fact, hens will eat just about anything.

Free-range farming produces healthier food and is kinder to the chickens, but a factory farm can produce much more food.

Most of the meat and eggs we eat are produced on large "factory farms", where the chickens are kept in cages, in special buildings called "battery houses".

Pig farming

Pigs give us bacon, pork, sausage meat, and ham. Their bristles are also used to make paint brushes. They are natural forest animals, and in some countries they used to roam wild in the woodlands.

Today, pigs usually live inside pig-pens and stalls, but in some countries they live outdoors, and they each have a little shelter.

If someone thinks something is untidy they will often say it is a "pig sty". Pigs are in fact very clean and tidy animals. The farmer gives them lots of straw, which they make into a cosy bed. In the morning, the pig will throw out any dirty straw. They never make a mess where they eat or sleep.

A female pig is called a **sow** and she will give birth to as many as twelve piglets, every three or four months. The babies are called a litter.

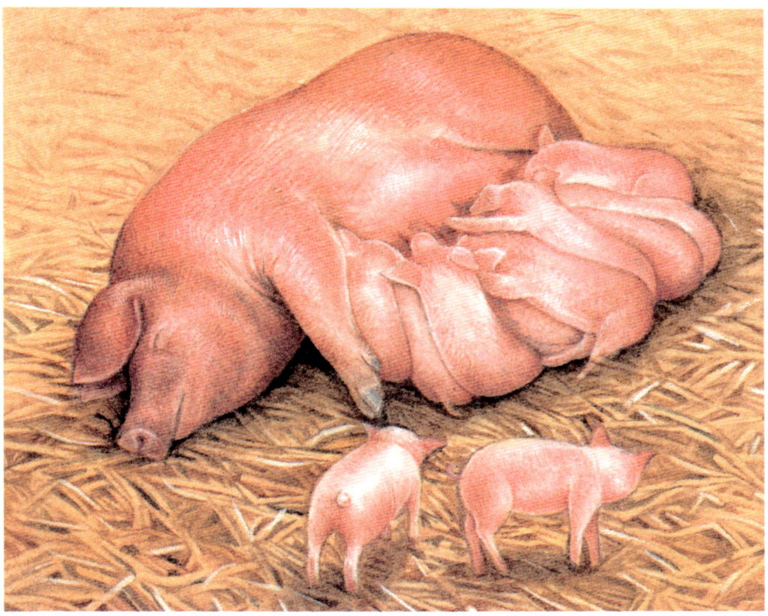

When the sow is ready to give birth, she will make a comfy straw bed, lie down, and give birth to the piglets. When a pig is having babies it is called **farrowing**.

The piglets each find one of their mother's teats and suckle happily. The strongest piglets get the best teats, with the best milk.

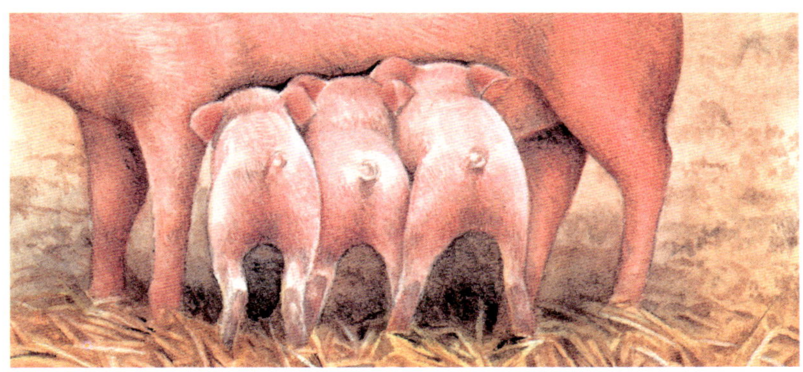

Farm Facts

Pigs do not sweat, so they roll around in the mud to keep cool.

Pigs have sensitive skins, so mud protects them from sunburn.

Ostrich farming

The ostrich is the world's largest living bird. Ostriches are farmed in various parts of the world to give us eggs, meat, and feathers. At the end of autumn, when the weather becomes cooler, the birds usually stop laying eggs.

Ostriches lay eggs every day during the warmer months. They usually lay in the late afternoon, not in the morning like hens. Some of the eggs will hatch into new chicks after six weeks.

Ostriches can grow to over 2 metres tall. Though they cannot fly, they can run at speeds of 64 kilometres per hour, which makes them the world's second-fastest animals. They are kept in a large fenced-off area, called a pen, which holds about 25 birds.

Farm Facts

Ostriches have a very short memory. They can only remember things for three seconds.

Ostrich skeletons have been found dating back over 200 million years. That makes the ostrich a living dinosaur!

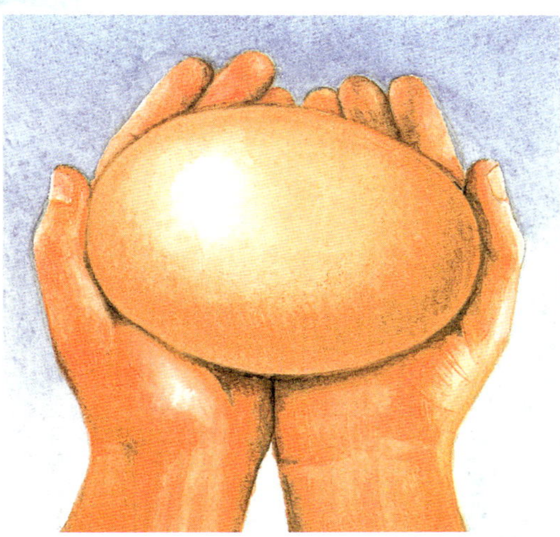

Ostriches lay the largest eggs of any bird. Each egg measures up to 20 cm. long and weighs 1.3 kg. An ostrich's egg has the volume of 40 chicken's eggs.

Fruit farming

Fruit gives us many of the vitamins we need to stay healthy, and you will see many different types of fruit in the supermarket today. In the autumn the trees in **orchards** are full of ripe apples and pears that are ready for harvest.

Apples and pears are picked by hand, so many fruit farms employ extra people to help with the harvest. Years ago, some families would travel from farm to farm to work during the picking season.

The pickers often need to climb ladders to reach the fruit, but some apple trees are so short that the apples can be reached from the ground.

Farm Facts

Pear trees are related to apple trees, but they are taller and last longer.

Most apples are grown for eating, others are grown for cooking or making apple juice and cider.

Most of the apples are cleaned and stored and taken to shops to be sold. Some farms will also sell their apples at the farm, and even let you "pick your own" fruit.

Today there are over 6,000 different types of apples. To create a new apple, the pollen from one kind of apple tree is dusted onto another. This produces an apple that is a mix of both types of tree.

Feeding and protecting the crops

Some crops, like wheat and barley, are strong enough to grow during the winter months, but the farmer needs to take care of them. The farmer will spray the growing crops with chemicals, which destroy harmful weeds or pests, but do not damage the crop.

The crops also need food to grow, so the farmer sprays chemical fertilizers over the field. The sprayer, which has long arms called booms, is pulled behind a tractor.

Organic farmers do not use chemical sprays. They use manure to fertilize the fields, using a machine called a spreader.

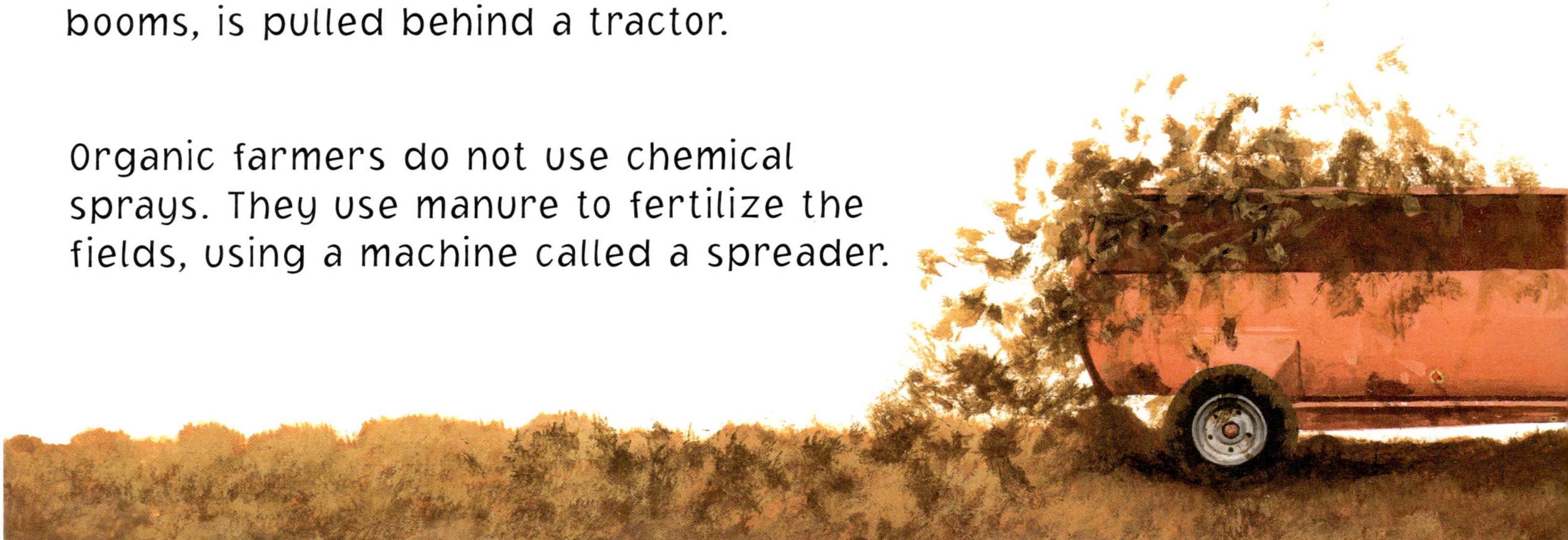

Farmers who grow vegetables or flowers may grow plants inside greenhouses or tunnels, which are made of strong, see-through plastic. Plants grown inside are kept warm and protected from the winter weather.

Farm Facts

Manure from cattle sheds, pigpens, and hen houses will be used to fertilize the fields.

Seaweed is another good natural fertilizer for crops.

Housing the animals

Any cattle still in the fields will be brought inside to cattle yards or sheds. The farmer gives them straw to sleep on, and feeds them with hay and silage that was made on the farm during the summer.

The farmer cleans the cattle sheds every day and the manure is stored in a pit. This manure will be used for fertilizing the fields.

As their woolly coats keep them warm, sheep can stay outside during winter. The farmer will take them extra food, like bales of hay and silage, every day.

Some of the female sheep, called ewes, will give birth to their lambs in the winter. The farmer brings them indoors to a shed where they are kept warm and dry.

Pigs can also live outside during the winter, if they have pigpens or huts to shelter in. The farmer takes them food and clean straw every day.

Chickens and hens can still live outdoors if they have a warm house to sleep in at night, or when it is too cold.

Farm Facts

Female pigs kept indoors may give birth to piglets during the winter.

Hens who live outdoors stop laying eggs in the winter, but start again in spring.

Fruit farming

In the winter, in some countries, the trees in the orchard will have lost their leaves and will need to have their branches cut back. This keeps the trees from growing too big and helps them grow more fruit in the next year. This is called "pruning".

It is also the time to plant new trees, which come from a special place called a "nursery". The new trees will start growing fruit about two years after they are planted.

In hotter parts of the world, such as Africa and Asia, farmers are still growing many types of fruit. The weather is different during the seasons around the world, which means there are fruit harvests almost all year round.

Florida, USA has one of the best growing climates for oranges. The warm sunshine produces lots of juicy fruit, that is full of nutrition. In the winter, the cooler weather makes the skin of the fruit turn a ripe orange-gold colour. This is when the Florida orange harvest begins.

Farm Facts

One orange tree can produce 1,000 oranges in a year.

Orange trees can produce fruit for 70 years or more.

Fish farming

Many types of fish are reared on special fish farms. These farms have ponds, lakes, or large tanks where the fish are kept. In the winter, the fish eggs hatch into tiny fish, called fish fry, and the farmer feeds them on special food, which helps them grow more quickly.

Some fish farms also have special nets or cages set up in the sea, where they can raise fish that like seawater.

As soon as they have grown bigger, the fish fry are moved into larger tanks or ponds and fed more food every day. This makes sure that the fish grow big and healthy.

The farm workers use nets to lift the fish out of the water. When the fish are moved from one place to another, they are taken in large tanks of water on the back of a tractor.

Farm Facts

Salmon and trout are two of the most popular farmed fish.

Some farms also grow shellfish, such as shrimp, lobster, or oysters.

Turkey farming

Think of the delicious smell of a turkey roasting in the oven at Christmas. Turkey farmers are busy raising birds all year round, but more people want turkeys for a traditional Christmas dinner, so winter is their busiest time.

A newly-hatched turkey chick is called a "poult". In the summer, the young poults are kept inside and given food and water by the farmer. They will stay inside until they are about five weeks old.

Some farms are free-range, which means the turkeys live in an open field and roam around in the fresh air and sunshine. There are also shelters in the field where they can sleep, and get shade when it is too hot.

Some turkeys are also raised on large factory farms where they are kept inside all the time.

Most turkeys are four months old when they are ready for harvest.

Farm Facts

Turkey feathers make a good natural fertilizer, so some farmers dig them back into the fields.

Turkey meat is believed to contain a natural chemical that causes sleepiress.

Christmas tree farms

Winter is the busiest time of year for Christmas tree farmers. The trees must be harvested and sold at this time, but it is a full-time, year-round job. Most Christmas trees are "conifers" or "evergreens". This is because they have "cones" and "needles," instead of leaves, which they keep all through the winter.

During the spring and summer, the farmer must control weeds, which take water and food away from the trees. Insects or disease can also harm the growing crop. A tree farmer must watch for this and remove, or cut back, any tree that is under attack.

Regular weed control, and cutting the grass between the rows of trees, keeps most tree crops healthy.

Once the trees are harvested, they are put through a special machine that covers the whole tree in netting. This protects the tree and makes it easier to handle.

Hundreds of trees will be loaded onto a big trailer and taken to the places where they are sold at Christmas.

Farm Facts

Christmas trees grow for 8 to 12 years before they are harvested.

There are over 600 different kinds of coniferous trees.

Repairs around the farm

Weather conditions around the world are different, so not all farms in all countries do the same jobs at the same time of year. Winter is usually the time when most repairs are done to machinery, buildings, fences, and all around the farm.

Leaves and twigs need to be cleaned out of the ditches around the fields. If they are blocked, the rain will not run away and the soil will become too muddy. Crops cannot grow if the soil is too wet. The farmer will clean out the ditches and dig new ones.

Walls and fences are needed to keep the animals in, and to protect the crops. The weather, animals, and age can damage them, so the farmer will fix any that are in need of repair.

Farm Facts

In the winter, the clocks are put back by one hour to give farmers more daylight hours to do their chores.

Frost can make stones and rocks come up in the soil. Some farmers use stone picking machines to remove them.

The farmer will also clean and check all the farm machinery to make sure it is working properly. Any repairs will be done so that everything is ready to use again in the spring.

Planning for next year

During the quieter winter months, the farmer will start planning for the next year. Most modern farmers keep their records and information on a computer. Computer records can tell the farmer how much milk each cow makes, or how well the crops grew in the summer.

Livestock farmers plan what animals they will keep. They also have to plan for the lambs and calves that will be born the following spring.

A crop farmer will decide which crops to grow and in which field. Farmers need to keep the soil fertile, which means that it is full of rich goodness to feed the crops. They do this by "rotating" the crops, which means they change the crops that grow in the fields.

A field that grew wheat last year might be planted with canola seed or corn for the coming year. It helps clear the field of any diseases, or pests, which may be in the soil from the previous crop.

Farm Facts

When a field has no crops planted in it, it is called a "fallow" field.

During winter, free-range hens stop laying eggs. Factory farms use e.ectric lights so the hens keep laying.

The farming year

Spring

- Preparing the soil for planting
- Planting the crops for harvest in the summer and autumn
- Fertilizing and protecting the crops
- Spring calving and lambing
- Animals put out to graze
- Milking dairy cows twice a day

Summer

- Watering crops
- Haymaking
- Harvesting cereal crops (wheat and barley)
- Harvesting soft fruit and vegetables
- Sheep shearing and dipping
- Making silage
- Cattle drives in the USA
- Milking dairy cows twice a day
- Agriculture fairs and farm shows

Autumn

- Ploughing the fields to prepare for planting
- Planting winter crops (wheat and barley)
- Harvesting potatoes, corn, and sugar beet
- Harvesting fruit (apples and pears)
- Sheep moved to new grazing land
- Milking dairy cows twice a day.
- Cattle brought indoors
- Hedge trimming

Winter

- Fertilizing and protecting the crops
- Housing the animals
- Pruning and planting of fruit trees
- Harvesting on turkey farms
- Harvesting on Christmas tree farms
- Milking dairy cows twice a day
- Repair fences, buildings, and machines
- Planning for next year

Glossary

Barley	This crop is ground down to make whiskey and beer.
Beef cattle	Cows kept for their meat.
Canola seed	Seed is crushed to make cooking oil and margarine.
Cattle farm	A farm that raises cows for their meat.
Climate	What the weather is like in an area or region.
Combine harvester	A machine that carries out all the jobs of the harvest.
Corral	Fenced-off area of a field, in USA
Crop farm	A farm that grows only grain crops.
Dairy cattle	Cows kept for their milk.
Dairy farm	A farm that raises cows for their milk.
Dibber	A stick that was used for planting seeds.
Ewe	A female sheep.
Farrowing	A sow giving birth to a litter of piglets.
Fertilizers	A chemical or natural product used to make crops grow better.
Flail	A stick that was used in harvesting to remove grain.
Fleece	The coat of a sheep or goat.
Flock	A group of sheep.
Furrow	New soil turned over by the plough.
Harrow	Tool used to smooth the soil.
Harvest	The gathering of the crops when ready.
Heft	Hill where sheep are kept.
Heifer	What a cow is called before she has her first calf.
Herbivores	Animals that eat only plants.
Herd	A group of cows.
Irrigation	Supplying the land with water by using pipes or channels.
Manure	Fertilizer made from animal dung and straw.
Nursery	A special place where plants are grown.

Orchard A farm where fruit trees are grown.
Organic farm A farm that grows crops without using chemicals.

Plough A machine that is used to prepare the soil for planting.
Pollution When harmful chemicals poison the Earth.
Poultry farm A farm that raises chickens, ducks, and geese.

Ram A male sheep.

Sap The sticky liquid that runs through trees.
Scythe A long-handled tool used to cut grass.
Seed bed Freshly ploughed soil where seeds are planted.
Seed drill A machine used to plant many seeds at once.
Shear To cut the wool off a sheep.
Sheaves A bundle of a gathered crop.
Sickle A short-handled tool used to cut grass.
Silage Animal food made using the natural chemicals in grass.
Silo Building used for storing animal feed.
Soil erosion When very dry soil is blown or washed away by wind or rain.
Sow A female pig.
Sugar beet A plant from which sugar is made.

Tap A hole made in a tree to get sap out.
Thresh To beat a crop to remove the grain from the husk.
Tilling Preparing the soil for planting.
Tilth Soil that is ready for planting.
Tractor A machine for lifting and pulling farm equipment.
Tuber The part of the potato plant that we eat.

Veterinary surgeon An animal doctor.

Weaning When a baby animal stops drinking its mother's milk and is fed by hand.
Wheat This crop is turned into flour to make bread.
Winnowing The action of tossing grain into the air to remove dust.

Index

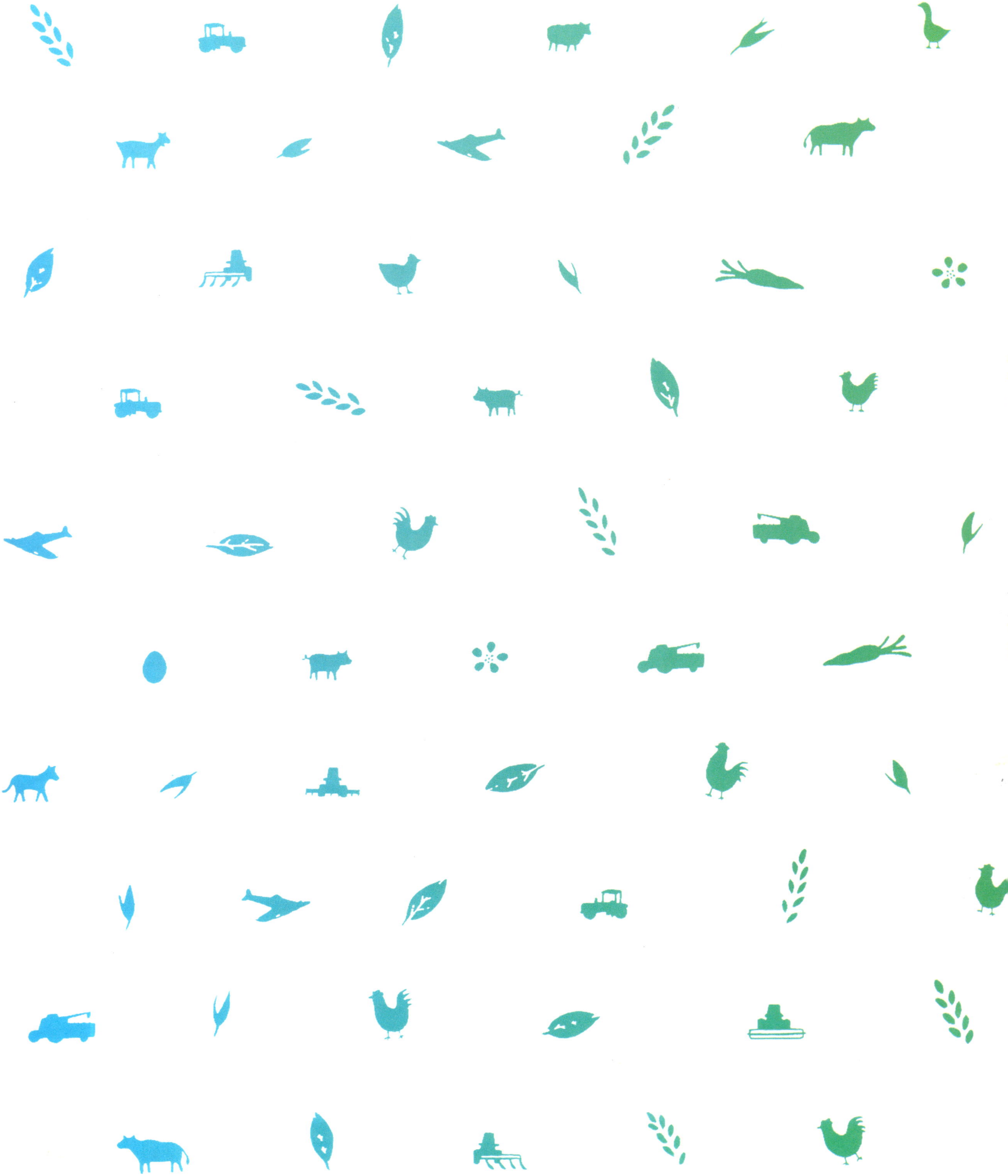